THIS BELONGS TO:

____

" IM CONVINCED THAT WE BLACK WOMEN POSSESS A SPECIAL INDESTRUCTIBLE STRENGTH THAT ALLOWS US TO NOT ONLY GET DOWN, BUT TO GET UP, TO GET THROUGH AND TO GET OVER."

- JANET JACKSON
SINGER, SONGWRITER

Day 1

What makes your soul feel free?

Day 2

What are your goals that will lead to your healing? How can you work towards those goals, in your everyday life?

Day 3

Society's standards of women can sometimes keep us in a box. List all the qualities about yourself that break that box.

Day 4

What's your definition of success?How do you measure your own success?

Day 5

Childhood traumas leak Into our adulthood, & often We don't even realize It. Do you think you've healed from them? Have you forgiven those who've caused you harm? Have you forgiven yourself for any mistakes you've made due to the long term effects of trauma?

"THE MOST COMMON WAY PEOPLE GIVE UP THEIR POWER IS BY THINKING THEY DON'T HAVE ANY."

– ALICE WALKER

NOVELIST, POET & SOCIAL ACTIVIST

DAY 6

USE THIS PROMPT TO WRITE DOWN EVERY POSITIVE ATTRIBUTE THAT YOU POSSESS.

TRY NOT TO THINK ABOUT WHAT OTHERS
HAVE ACKNOWLEDGED YOU FOR,
BUT WHAT YOU ACKNOWLEDGE
WITHIN YOURSELF.

Day 7

How strong Is your stance when honoring your boundaries? Are there any parts of your life that lack In boundaries?

Day 8

What do you value most In friendships? Do you represent those same values In your own Friendships?

Day 9

The essence of black beauty runs deep, and it's vital for that to be implemented within our childhood. How we perceive ourselves mostly depends on how we were raised. Who do you see when you look in the mirror? In what ways do you feel your upbringing instilled the values of black beauty? In what ways would you say there wasn't as much of a presence with this then, that you're aware of now?

DAY 10

WRITE A LETTER TO SOMEONE WHO YOU FORGAVE, BUT THEY NEVER APOLOGIZED.

DAY 11

HAVE YOU AVOIDED ANYTHING THIS WEEK?

"I was built this way for a reason, so I'm going to use It."

- Simone Biles

American Gymnast

DAY 12

GIVEN THE CHANCE, WOULD YOU UNDO ANY WRONGS? OR HAVE YOU ACCEPTED THE PAST, AND MOVED FORWARD?

DAY 13

WHAT MAKES YOU FEEL SAFE?

Day 14

WHAT LESSONS/VALUES HAVE YOU OBTAINED ON YOUR OWN THAT YOU WISH YOUR PARENTS GAVE TO YOU EARLIER IN LIFE? DO YOU RESENT THEM FOR IT?

Day 15

Power of the tongue ladies. Create affirmations that you'll live by to consistently polish your Inner self. Be Intentional!

Day 16

Are there things that you blame yourself for? Is It fair to put the blame on your shoulders?

DAY 17

FOCUS ON ANY
NEW SELF DISCOVERIES YOU'VE MADE.
WHAT ARE THEY? WHAT WAS
YOUR MOMENT OF REALIZATION?

"You are your best thing."

- Toni Morrison

NOVELIST, BOOK EDITOR, COLLEGE PROFESSOR

Day 18

It's time to address the elephant In the room and thats bad habits! We all have them. What came to mind? Think about the work It'll take to break those habits.

Day 19

What has been the most difficult part of your growing pains?
How did you overcome that?

Day 20

Describe your Ideal life. Who Is this version of you? What are their strengths? What are you doing to achieve that, and make It your reality?

Day 21

Based on personal experiences what comes to mind when you think of defense mechanisms vs suppression? If any, whats the correlation?

Day 22

As black women, we suffer circumstances most would never understand. How do you think that's molded you Into who you are today?

Day 23

What does It take for you to express vulnerability? Does It come to you naturally? Do you struggle? Assess your vulnerability, what does It say about your emotional/mental health?

"WE MUST REJECT NOT ONLY THE STEREOTYPES THAT OTHERS HOLD OF US, BUT ALSO THE STEREOTYPES THAT WE HOLD OF OURSELVES."

- SHIRLEY CHISHOLM

POLITICAN, EDUCATOR, AUTHOR

Day 24

An ugly truth no one warned you about was?

Day 25

What unhealthy attachments (people/places/things)do you hold onto? Are you afraid of letting go? Think about what you'd gain from taking action to cutting those ties.

Day 26

Do you guard your heart out of wisdom or pain? Why?

Day 27

What is your definition of sexual liberation?
How Important Is that to you?

Day 28

As beautiful as love Is, It Is never an easy thing to handle. truly a rollercoaster ride. Think about all your experiences with Love, how has It changed you? In what ways have you grown? was self love a priority ?

Day 29

On your next day off, create the perfect self care day at home. Your definition of self care Is exclusive to you, go all out! When you're done, or a day after take time to reflect here on what you did that day. Maybe you can try this routine again on a day you're not feeling your best self.

Day 30

Leave your book at home, take yourself on a date. Plan It out, spoil yourself. Reflect on how It went when you come home.

"The only thing that's gonna fix your life, Is you loving yourself."

- Mary J. Blige

SINGER,SONGWRITER

www.ingramcontent.com/pod-product-compliance
Ingram Content Group UK Ltd.
Pitfield, Milton Keynes, MK11 3LW, UK
UKHW021528300726
14060UKWH00011B/28

9 786277 544058